Darknet S

A Beginner's Underground Playbook To
The Secrets Of Staying Anonymous Online

Yuri A. Clarke

Table Of Contents:

Introduction

It all started with a simple question and an Internet connection. You see, I have been using the Internet for my entire life. I have seen the rise and fall of websites, software, and memes. I saw the Internet grow from its infancy when MSN was the Messenger of the '90s. I remember the good old YouTube format. I can say that I have seen it all. In fact, I have seen things that only a few people get to see: privacy invasion over the Internet.

I was very much like every other user on the Internet – oblivious to how things were developing all around me. It all started about five years ago when I noticed something funny on Facebook. I love making online purchases because of the convenience it provides. However, when I started looking for second-hand furniture to decorate my living room, I was bombarded with even more advertisements for furniture. If they were burgers or coke ads, then I would not have noticed. However, furniture advertisements were very unusual because I had never seen them before in my news feed. It was then I realized that something was up. I went through my news feed and carefully considered what I had posted on Facebook. Surely enough, every single advertisement I had seen on Facebook was related to my interests, in one way or another. It wasn't a huge deal because they were just advertisements. I had enough self-restraint not to buy literally everything I saw online. However, that incident got me thinking: how were these advertisements so smart?

And so, I went and did a little digging. One simple question led to another, and then three, then five, then ten more. Before long, I realized that I had learned of something big that I felt must be shared with everyone. This is why I have written this book.

Our privacy is compromised. Now, some people may not care too much about their privacy. I can respect that. However, I once got into trouble as a kid when my parents went through my diary and asked me questions. Since then, I have never kept a diary. You see, I never really liked the idea of having someone watching everything that I do, even though I have no reason to hide it. Do you find it uncomfortable when you are at your desk, and someone just stands right there behind you, observing your every move? I don't like that feeling. Now, I had the same feeling when I learned of what governments, social networking sites, websites, and organizations had been doing with my private data.

It wouldn't be that big a deal still if they keep it for legitimate research purposes. In fact, I'm willing to share it. However, those entities cross the line when they used my data to manipulate my behavior and opinions. I don't like it when they sell shoes to me at a higher price just because I buy them often. I hate the fact that airplane tickets are more expensive just because of my geographical location. Most importantly, I hate it when these entities collect all my data without asking my permission or making it hard for me to understand how they handle my private data. There are companies out there that actively monitor and collect private data from you and sell it to third parties without your knowledge.

That's not all. I have also read about governments that actively spy on their own citizens and attempt to silence political dissents and whistleblowers. Those people were either dead, arrested, missing, or powerless and voiceless. I hasten to add - were. There is hope for us all to take back our fundamental right to privacy, which is the core of freedom of speech that we all deserve.

And this is why I wrote this book. I want to raise awareness of this privacy issue to as many people as possible and tell you exactly how you can wrestle back control of your privacy.

I will tell you all that you need to know about data privacy, its importance, how companies are violating it, as well as how you can remain anonymous online so that you can browse the "cleanest" Internet, free from watchful eyes of the government and other organization looking to steal your data.

You don't need to be a tech geek to protect yourself. I will provide you with a clear, step-by-step guide as to how you can protect yourself online. Are you ready to take back your right to privacy? Then read on.

Chapter 1: Welcome To The Dark Side Of The Internet

What Is Data Privacy?

Data privacy, also known as information privacy, is all about how your data is handled by your Internet service provider (ISP). That includes your consent to having your data shared with third parties such as the government or other companies, notice, and regulatory obligations on the part of the provider. To be exact, data privacy revolves around:

1. Whether or how data is shared with third parties

2. How data is legally collected or stored

3. Regulations that set restrictions on data handling

Why Do You Need Data Privacy?

If you go to Google Chrome now and turn to go incognito, you will be greeted with a disclaimer. It is explicitly stated that your browsing history, cookies, and site data, as well as information entered in forms through the incognito tab, will not be saved. However, the website that you visit can still see your activity. If you use incognito at work or school, then your activities can still be tracked. Even your Internet service provider knows what website you visited and when.

Incognito or other built-in private solutions your browser provides only serve to save you the hassle of deleting your browsing history. They do not grant you full anonymity. So why is anonymity important?

There are two main reasons why you should be worried about what data your ISP collects from you.

You see, data is perhaps one of the most valuable assets a company has. With it, they can create an advertisement that answers your likes and dislikes, which increases the chance of getting your interests and engagement. Right now, data is more valuable than ever before because companies use this to train their bots to respond to your activities. For example, when you go to YouTube, all the videos you see in there are all related to what you have watched. The bots bring relevant videos to you based on what you have watched in the past. That is not to say anything about the use of data to sway public opinions on political matters.

Another reason why data privacy is important is surveillance. You don't want anyone to spy on you, do you? No one wants the government to breathe down their necks. A common argument you see here is, "If you didn't do anything wrong, you have nothing to hide." Edward Snowden, who was seemingly forgotten for his deed on exposing the US NSA program which spied on civilians, responded to this statement in an interview with John Oliver in Last Week Tonight by saying that it was hardly any different to holding a gun to someone's head and telling them to trust you because you won't pull the trigger. Privacy is one of those things that should be left well alone unless absolutely necessary.

No one can live comfortably knowing that someone is watching your every move and knows everything about you. Privacy is one of our most important needs.

Who Endangers Your Data Privacy And What Are The Risks?

Unfortunately, in this day and age, it is becoming increasingly harder for you to protect your own data and privacy. As previously stated, turning on the incognito mode will not provide sufficient anonymity. Your Internet service provider can still track your activities. In case of a criminal investigation, the government can force your ISP to share your data. If the law allows it, you can be sure that your ISP will sell your data at the drop of a hat. In fact, some ISP offer a costlier package for additional data protection. It basically means that your ISP promises not to sell your data to third-party companies if you subscribe to this service. Companies can track your activities on their website and use this data to (sometimes aggressively) push annoying advertisements your way. If you do not watch your step, criminal entities can steal your data, such as your passwords and compromise your online accounts across the board if you use the same password for all your accounts.

Anonymity

So, what you need is anonymity. Anonymity is like putting on a mask. Your activities may still be recorded, but there is no way to trace them back to you. Your identity is protected from being shared with other people online. There are many levels of anonymity. For instance, you have secure billing which protects your personal information from being shared with the distributor and other online interaction sites such as Omegle, 4Chan, or Formspring which allow you to interact, network, post, or even flirt with other users while remaining anonymous (hence the term "anon").

Why Is Anonymity Important?

Anonymity is a widely contested topic. Some people believe that it is of utmost importance, as stated earlier. Others believe that everyone's activities should be tracked so as to discourage undesirable behaviors. While both arguments are valid, some of the biggest questions here are: Is the complete sacrifice of privacy, the only way to curb criminal behavior? Is there really no other way? Is it worth it?

That said, there are three main reasons why anonymity is important.

Identity Protection

Sometimes, the answer is very simple. You just don't want people to know who you are when you visit a website, even if you are not doing anything illegal or questionable. This is something that many people would find very helpful and comforting. There are certain things that should just be kept a secret.

Here's an extreme case, although not far from the truth. Imagine that you are a world-class celebrity who won multiple Oscar awards over the past few years. At that level of fame, you can expect the paparazzi to be all over your place 24/7. It can be annoying and tiresome, can't it? Celebrities like those cherish all the little privacy they can get, especially online. A statement about any sensitive issues will be the end of their careers, although they only intended to generate discussion.

Anonymity is something that you take for granted until you no longer have it.

A good example is South Korea, with its resident registration number. All residents have a unique code assigned to them. This code serves as an identifier and is needed to register for online accounts, including websites, games, etc.

This sounds like a good idea because you can then limit one person to only having one account per service. However, what if those codes are leaked?

You don't have to answer that. It happened in 2006.

It was part of a money-laundering operation that affected hundreds of thousands of registration numbers, which were used to create false accounts in Lineage, an online computer game. The kicker here is that those numbers were not hacked. They were sold by the company employees who had database-access.

Having your banking information compromised is bad, but it is nothing that you cannot rectify. You just need to provide proof of identification, and the bank will handle everything for you. The registration, however, is equivalent to your ID card. Having your whole identity stolen and compromised can be disastrous.

Personal Harassment

Freedom of expression is only going to work when full anonymity is guaranteed. In a government that actively tries to suppress dissents, anonymity is one of the only protection civilians and whistle-blowers alike have to defend themselves with. They need to find a way to express discontent with the government without being arrested, so anonymity is key.

But harassment is not limited to politics. Online harassment can come in many forms, including:

1. Doxing: All your personal information is released to the public for use, including name, address, email, professional profiles, etc. This can result in pranks, stalkers, or even death threats.

2. Swatting: Swatting is a very serious problem among online streamers. As its name suggests, it occurs when someone wrongly and intentionally calls the SWAT team to storm your home and arrest you. At best, you'll be released with minor injuries. At worse? Death. It's not at all rare to see someone being shot because they reacted incorrectly when they were being swatted.

3. Revenge porn: When intimate relationships go sour, some people turn to revenge porn. That means releasing intimate photos or videos of you on the Internet without your knowledge or consent.

However, the protection that allows you to speak your mind is still important in situations that are not as serious as what we have just described. For instance, some people argue that the world would be a better place if people were held accountable for what they say. However, the opposite is also true. With freedom of speech, people are more willing to be truthful about their own thoughts and feelings, especially when they have something negative to say.

Here's another example. Suppose that you live in a dangerous neighborhood that is plagued with gang activities. You read about a news article and found out about yet another fatal shooting incident. You wanted to speak your mind on the matter, but fear that the gang in your neighborhood will find out about it and attempt to silence you. You can speak out if you have anonymity.

Whistleblowing is an extreme example because you essentially expose a major corporation or even the government. The risk is clear as day. Without anonymity, there will be dangerous consequences of releasing sensitive information and evidence to the public.

Sensitive Issues

Anonymity has one more use. For instance, suppose that you want to find information about a certain topic, but do not want to be seen doing it. Many people actually fall into this group, hence the ongoing joke about deleting the browsing history or turning on incognito mode.

For instance, some people question and want to understand their own sexuality and do not want to come out of the closet yet. They may not even be sure if they are what they think they are, and there are many questions they want to be answered. That person can go to an online community and find out more information without revealing their identity.

Another example is people finding out about their medical information. A person might want to find out about their funny bowel movements. Young girls want to find out more about teen pregnancy or STI and perhaps even seek out medical advice or services without alerting their parents about it. These people can do that while remaining anonymous.

As you can see, the list goes on and on endlessly. People can seek help for their personal issues without revealing their identity. Many people have taken this for granted. How would you feel if all the questions you asked on the Internet were revealed and traced back to you?

What Is The Dark Web?

In short, the dark web is a place where your anonymity is guaranteed, if you follow the correct procedure to set things upright. Many people associate the dark web to the black market for good reasons. If you were to go to the dark web, you could find a marketplace for drugs and human traffickers. That is terrible, but this is also a safe haven for political dissents and whistleblowers.

The dark web makes up roughly 6% of the Internet in terms of content. You cannot just access it on Google Chrome or other common browsers you can think of. You need specific software and configuration to access this dark area.

To help you put things into perspective, there are three levels of the web. Surface web, deep web, and dark web.

The surface web contains all the things you can find on Google or other browsers, hence the term "surf the web." It only makes up about 4% of Internet content.

The deep web comprises the largest portion of the Internet, with up to 90% share of content. It is the area that the search engine cannot reach and comprises things such as IP addresses, domains, and internal networks, among others that you cannot access with your Internet browser. The deep web is not the dark web, however.

The dark web is perhaps as deep as the Internet can go. You can only access it using specific software and configuration. Here, everyone literally goes dark, and anonymity is guaranteed. With this anonymity, people can purchase illegal drugs, weapons, or even other humans.

However, that does not mean it is a place for cutthroat criminals. There are other legitimate sites on the dark web. The only difference between that and the surface web is anonymity, and some people just want to feel safe when chatting with other people. It is a safe haven for journalists and whistleblowers, as well. So really, you can see the dark web as the most powerful tool to combat censorship.

So here is the big question: Why does the dark web seem like such a bad place? It is not that bad considering the facts that we have here. Well, you have the mainstream media to thank for that.

Perhaps what gave the Dark Web a bad reputation was the emergence and subsequent discovery of the Silk Road, a massive drug-dealing depot, back in 2011. Its value was estimated to be at $2.4 billion at its peak in 2013. When the US government finally managed to find the founder and promptly shut down Silk Road, the mainstream media jumped to conclusions and wrote extensively about how the Dark Web was a place for criminals to do their dirty business.

Ross Ulbricht, the creator of Silk Road, argued that the website was actually intended for people to buy and sell merchandise without worrying about the tax or delayed delivery thanks to state intervention. Unfortunately, his explanation was predictably censored to the rest of the world, and only a few people caught onto the idea.

As of now, the mainstream media has been scaremongering everyone into thinking that the Dark Web is a forbidden zone. It is pretty much the opposite. According to James Chappel, CTO, and Co-Founder of Digital Shadows, which is a global company that monitors online risk across the Internet, all 3 levels of them, 95% of the sites in the dark web, are harmless. Many people assume that everything on the dark web is illegal, and they don't want to have anything to do with it. James went on to explain that the Dark Web, as we have argued, serves as a sanctuary where people can get the privacy they need. To him, privacy is a human right that must not be violated. He believes that surveillance is a threat to democracy.

To sum it all up, the Dark Web is not as bad as anyone would think. It is undeniable that there are criminal activities going on in the Dark Web, but you can say the same thing on the surface web. Some sites serve as a host for some illegal activities such as software or document distribution. Being able to purchase illegal drugs, weapons, or other humans is bad, but it is just as illegal to be downloading books, songs, software, or eBooks online without paying for it. In fact, there are more people downloading free things than there are drug dealers.

Mainstream media, tech companies, and government agencies have been doing their best to label the Dark Web as a dark and forbidden zone. To their credit, they did a great job of manipulating the public. However, people are becoming increasingly aware of the lies and becoming more worried about their own privacy in the comfort of their own home. Thanks to the courageous few who advocate for the use of the Dark Web, the idea that it is a safe haven where privacy is guaranteed is slowly emerging.

In reality, the Dark Web has a lot of potentials. It can even be the future of the Internet as a whole. Because the government has no power there, everyone would be free from surveillance. Those who have lost their voice can find it in the Dark Web, and there will be people to listen to them. Without the government's influence over the citizens, the people can finally have the freedom of speech. To top it all off, people can do it with impunity because their identity is hidden. If there are enough people in the Dark Web, then it can be as vast as the abyss itself. The Dark Web shall serve as a place where everyone is truly free from any sort of influence. It is an Internet paradise where you can find just about anything.

Chapter 2: Understanding The Tor-Network

Introduction

The Tor network is a group of servers operated by volunteers with two goals in mind: privacy and security on the Internet. Tor users simply connect through virtual tunnels, which literally made them go dark. Through this virtual tunnel, their data go through to their destination rather than going straight to the destination and getting tracked. With this virtual tunnel, organizations and individuals alike can access the Internet and communicate with each other without getting their security or privacy compromised.

But there is another use for Tor. It is a powerful tool to combat censorship because the users can bypass the blockage and access the data behind it.

Because Tor is open-source, software developers can use it to build new communication tools with powerful privacy features built-in from Tor.

Ordinary individuals use Tor mainly to keep sites or other service providers from tracking their activities. This opens up for the possibilities of communication that other providers cannot, such as that on sensitive issues we mentioned previously.

Political dissidents, journalists, and whistleblowers can use Tor to communicate with each other safely. NGOs also employ Tor to communicate when they are operating inside a foreign country to eliminate the risk of having their identity revealed.

TOR is an effective tool against surveillance because of the wide variety of people who use it. The more people there are in the network, the more secure the connection is. You see, your activities are mixed in with that of others on the network, so tracking any particular data packet is outright impossible.

Why You Need Tor?

TOR protects its users from traffic analysis, which is a form of Internet surveillance. Traffic analysis can be used to determine who is talking to whom in a public network. When you know the source and destination of a person's Internet traffic, tracking their behavior and interests should be relatively easy. With this information, an e-commerce shop owner can jack up the price for sportswear for those who are interested in sports or simply increase the price for those living in different regions of the world.

Traffic analysis can even be used to reveal who and where you are, therefore threatening your job and physical security. For instance, if you are on holiday and check your business email, you immediately reveal your nationality and professional profile to anyone who happens to observe the network, even if the connection itself is encrypted.

But before we can understand how Tor comes into play, we need to understand the threats posed by traffic analysis first. You see, the Internet data packet has two parts. Think of your data packet as mail. Contained inside the mail is whatever you want to send, and you write where you want the mail to be delivered. The same thing applies to the data packet. You have the data payload and the header. The payload is the data that needs to be sent, and the header is used to direct the data to its destination. Even with encryption, it will only protect the payload itself and not the header. So when you send a data packet out, be it an email, message, or movie clip, traffic analysis can still reveal a lot about you and what you are doing. Depending on the data packet sent, it could even tell what you were saying. Traffic analysis targets the header because it shows the packet's source, destination, size, timestamps, etc.

You can see the issue with the open Internet here. The recipient, the one you are communicating with, can see what you sent by looking at the headers. That is not so much of a problem. The problem is that there are third-parties such as your ISP, or other organizations or individuals, who can gather such information. The simplest form of traffic analysis is to sit between the sender and recipient and monitor the data package by looking at the headers.

To make matters worse, there are more powerful traffic analysis tools. Some attackers deployed a vast net of surveillance by spying on many parts of the Internet and gather all the information before piecing it all together, using advanced statistical techniques to reveal communication patterns of many organizations or individuals. Again, encryption only protects the package itself, not the header.

Brief History Of Tor

With the continuous growth of the Internet in the 1990s, society was transformed on a global scale. Among those changes was the rise of instant communication.

It can take months for a letter to reach someone on the other side of the planet in the old days. But thanks to the Internet, you can send messages instantaneously. So long as both parties are connected to the Internet, they can talk to each other with ease. By 2000, there were over 350 million users. Since then, there was a concern about the growth of the Internet. You see, the Internet was never designed to grant anonymity to its users.

This seems sensible because the authority can properly conduct criminal investigations; people started to become concerned about their privacy. Among those concerned parties was the US federal government.

Then, a group of mathematicians and computer scientists from the Naval Research Laboratory (NRL) started the development of a new technology that allows for anonymous bi-directional communication. This means that the destination and the source of the communication cannot be determined by a mid-point.

With this technology, the US government created a system that allows completely anonymous communication on the Internet. However, there was a caveat. In order for anonymity to work, they need to flood the system with other users. It makes no sense to wear a mask to conceal your identity when everyone else cannot wear it, after all. Everyone will know that it is you. The same thing can be said for technology. If the US agents were authorized to use this technology, whereas no one in public can, then whenever these agents go into a website, everyone could tell that it is the US government looking through their site, which defeats the purpose of anonymity. Therefore, the technology must be released to the public.

Because of this, the NRL released the Tor browser, their onion routing technology. Tor stands for The Onion Router, and this is your key to the network of onion routers, the dark web itself. As of now, there are millions of users using the Tor browser. With Tor released to the public under a free license, the Tor Project was founded as a non-profit organization. It exists to this day thanks to the financial support of the Electronic Frontier Foundation as well as many other organizations.

How Tor Works

Tor protects you from traffic analysis by redirecting your data all over the place, literally. That way, no matter where your data is intercepted, they cannot tell where it is going or where it comes from. It is like trying to throw off someone who has been following you by going into a building and then changing your clothes or appearance before leaving the building. You do that multiple times, and it becomes impossible to track you.

So when you send out a data packet, it does not go to its destination directly. Instead, it goes through random pathways through several relays, so your tracks are covered, and no one at any stage of the traffic can tell where the data came from or where it is going.

In order to create a private network pathway, the Tor client on your computer creates a circuit of encrypted connection going through multiple relays on the network. The circuit is only extended from one relay to the next, or one data hop at a time. The relays themselves do not reveal the final destination of the data. They only tell the data's source and the next destination (the next relay). Even if one relay is compromised, the attacker does not have complete information about the data traffic. Moreover, the Tor client itself creates a separate set of encryption keys for each hop to each relay along its path, so these connections cannot be traced.

After a circuit has been created, your data can safely pass through the Tor network safely. Again, because each relay only sees one hop in the entire circuit, it is impossible for attackers to see the entire circuit. It is worth noting that Tor only works for TCP streams, and any application with SOCKS support can use it.

For the sake of efficiency, Tor uses the same circuit for connection within the same ten minutes. Any other connections outside this period will follow a new circuit, so your anonymity is secured.

Node Types

To make the most out of Tor, you need to run a Tor relay. Not only that, a Tor relay is faster, but it is also more robust against attacks, more stable, and safer for you. All the nodes are important for securing your connection, but they have different requirements as well as legal implications. Therefore, you need to understand the three main kinds of nodes so you can understand which one suits your needs.

First, we have the Guard Node, which can see your IP address but does not know what data you are sending out because of the encryption layer. The Guard Node is also known as the entry node. This node knows that you send your data through Tor, and it needs to pass the data through to the next server.

Middle servers are all the nodes in the middle between the Guard Node and the Exit Node. These nodes can do little other than to pass the data on to the next node in the circuit. It can only decrypt one layer of encryption before passing on the data. It cannot read the data payload, and it does not know the source or destination of the data.

Finally, the Exit Node. It is the final node your data needs to pass through before reaching its true destination. The Exit Node has access to the data payload because it removes the final layer of encryption before sending the data to the website or recipient. However, it cannot tell where the data came from originally. It can only tell which middle server it received the data from.

Chapter 3: The "Hidden" .Onion Service

Definition

Onion routing is a communication protocol for devices to transmit and receive data anonymously. Here, all data are protected by multiple layers of encryption, which gives the name. This encrypted data is then sent through a series of network nodes known as onion routers. Upon arrival at each node, the node decrypts the outer layer of the encryption. Think of it as peeling the layer of an onion. This decryption does not reveal much about the data content other than where it is heading to next. And so, the data is sent to the next node, peeled, rinse, and repeat until the final layer is removed upon arrival. The sender the data is anonymous because each node knows the previous and next destination of the data. Unfortunately, even with this level of security, the onion routing technique still has its vulnerabilities.

Data Structure

Onion routing protects your data by encrypting the message, the data payload, over and over again to create layers of protection. Such encryptions can only be decrypted layers by layers as the data arrives at its intermediary nodes or computers. The payload remains secured as each node cannot extra the data from the payload. All that the node knows is the data's source and destination, and it can only pass the data along to the adjacent node for the next decryption process. The entire process continues until the message arrives at its destination, so the sender of the data remains anonymous.

In order for this transmission of data to be successful, the nodes through with your data go through are chosen at random from a directory node, which is basically a database of all available nodes for use. All the chosen nodes form a path, and this is how your data is transmitted. In order to protect your anonymity, each node has the capacity to fully decrypt your data to find out whether the data it just received came from you or a fellow intermediary node. Moreover, no node in the entire system knows how many nodes your data will go through. There is only one node that knows that it is the final node in the entire chain. It is called the exit node.

However, the path that your data goes through, or the circuit, is not as simple. First, to send encrypted data to the first node, you need to establish a connection with it. To do that, your device access the directory node to retrieve a public key. With it, your device can connect to the first node and create a connection session. By using the encrypted connection to the entry node, you can then send your data to it. However, the entry node can only receive your data and pass it on to the next node because only the next node can decrypt the outermost layer of encryption.

When the first node made a connection with the second node, your data is ready to be passed on. In doing so, your encrypted link will be extended to the second node. This process repeats itself until the data finally reaches the exit node and is sent to its final destination. Normally, the data is passed through 3 nodes before the destination. You can increase the number of nodes in the circuit if you want, but your connection will be very slow due to all the redirecting needed.

Anyway, after the chain is complete, as in the link has been established among all the nodes and to the host website, you can then send data over anonymously. The host website can see the data coming from the exit node, but cannot determine the data's actual source. The recipient of the data can send the data back to you, starting with the exit node. So the roles reverse, and your exit node becomes the entry node, and the entry node becomes the exit node. The encryption and decryption process still occur as previously described, finishing up with the exit node (initially the entry node) decrypting the data before handing it to you.

Weaknesses

Even with such a complicated process, onion routing is not invulnerable. Given time and resources, it can still be cracked. The main reason why the Internet is not anonymous is that your ISP can track and log connections between devices. For instance, when you go to Amazon, your data may be sent through a secured connection like HTTPS, so your emails, password, or other information are hidden from third-parties. However, they can still collect a record of the connection, such as the time as well as the data transferred from your device to the site itself.

The onion routing technique attempts to combat this problem by preventing the connection record. It does this by obscuring the connection path between you and the website. Because there are so many users and circuits to monitor, tracking down any particular connection and linking it from the website back to any individual user is difficult. However, that can still be done because the connection between nodes can still be recorded.

One weakness of the onion routing technique is what is called timing analysis. Basically, it goes through all records of connection across all nodes and looks at the time and data size, both of which are not hidden, of the data sent between nodes. For example, you can change the timing of the data based on a certain pattern and then look for that pattern on the other side of the network. Another example is when you see that one computer sends 100kb of data to another unknown computer and that unknown computer sends the same amount of data to another website. So it is not very difficult to infer the source and destination of a connection, even if it is protected by onion routing.

Other factors that increase the effectiveness of traffic analysis are when a node fails and leaves the network or when it is compromised so that it keeps track of all traffic going through it.

Another weakness of the onion router is called Exit node vulnerability, which is potentially the biggest flaw of the onion router. You see, even though your messages are shielded behind several layers of encryption, the exit node is the one to decrypt the final protective layer and send the message to your recipient. I'm sure you can see the problem here.

If you can identify the exit node and compromise it somehow, you immediately have access to the payload, the content of the data itself that could include passwords, messages, or other sensitive information.

If an attacker can pull that off, then your data is as secured as sending it through an unsecured public Wi-Fi where it can be easily intercepted by other users or the router operator. You can solve this problem by adding another layer of protection. You can do this by using a secure end-to-end connection such as S-HTTP or SSL. Without the end-to-end encryption between you and the recipient and you do not trust a wrong SSL certificate that the exit node gave you, then there is no way of seeing your message even if the exit node is compromised.

Chapter 4: Hiding Tor-Traffic Inside Encrypted Tunnels

VPNs can seem scary and complicated at first. In reality, it is very easy to use and set up. A Virtual Private Network allows you to surf the web anonymously by running your connection through the VPN server and hiding your activities. But how does it work in practice?

How Does A VPN Work?

A VPN works a bit differently from a Tor network. It all begins when you launch a VPN client and proceed to connect to the Internet through the client. Whether you are going online on your private network or public, your data is encrypted as it leaves your device. That means even your ISP cannot see it. The data goes through the VPN first then to a VPN server, before reaching its destination. On the other end, the receiver of your data only sees that it came from a VPN server and the server's location, not yours.

Without a VPN, anyone can intercept your data packet and see what's inside, including where it came from (your computer), where it's going (a website), and the content of the packet. The Internet is a bunch of interconnected servers that communicate with each other all the time. They share your information across the servers to facilitate your browsing of the web. However, that leaves you vulnerable to attackers.

Think of going online as going on a flight on a commercial airline. You share your personal information with the ticket agent, baggage handler, security personnel, and the flight attendants throughout the entire flight. The same thing is happening on the open Internet.

If you are just browsing blog sites or other fun pages, then you have nothing to worry about. Even if someone sees that you have been there, they cannot do much with this information. However, you should be concerned if it is about your banking account, business emails, or other sensitive information.

So when you use a VPN server, your data is encrypted. That is done to protect attackers from knowing what you send. Even when your data comes under attack, the attacker can only tell that the packet came from your computer and to a VPN server. From this server, your data is passed forward to its destination. It protects your privacy and guarantees security for four main reasons:

1. The host site can only see your data coming from a VPN server, not you

2. Tracing your data back to you is difficult, if not outright impossible

3. Even if someone intercepts your data, they cannot see what you are sending

Again, this is in theory. But how does VPN fare in practice?

How Secure Is A VPN?

This is a contentious issue because no two VPN service providers are the same. It all comes down to two things:

1. The VPN technology used by the provider and its inherent limitation

2. Legal and policy limitations that influence what the provider can do with the technology

Speaking of legal and policy limitations...

Is The Use Of A VPN Legal?

The short answer is "yes." The long answer is "not always." You see, the legislation has a hard time keeping up with the advancement of technology. Take Bitcoin, for example. Everyone knows about it now, and yet governments are doing very little to regulate it. The same can be said for the VPN.

Because some jurisdictions are underdeveloped in the technology field, that means existing law is open to interpretation. But overall, the use of a VPN is legal in most countries, especially in Canada, the US, and Europe. VPN is definitely not recommended for use in China, Iraq, Turkey, United Arab Emirates, Belarus, Oman, Iran, Russia, North Korea, and Turkmenistan. It is worth pointing out that what matters is your physical location when you use a VPN. That means you cannot use it when you are in Russia, even though your exit location is in America. The reverse is perfectly safe.

In short, make sure to check with the legality of VPN in your own country by going through the laws of your government.

How To Install A VPN On A Router

Installing a VPN on your router is highly recommended, as that means all traffic going through your router would be encrypted. That also means that you don't need to install applications individually on your devices.

So first, make sure that your router supports VPN. You can check that by going to the site of the manufacturer that produced the router. DD-WRT, Tomato-booster FlashRouters are usually compatible with VPNs. You also need to check out the website of the VPN service providers themselves to check out how to set up a VPN with your router.

In short, you just need to log into your router and then fill out some simple forms. You do not need to be tech-savvy to pull this off.

Logging Policies

Again, the level of anonymity your VPN provides depends on how they log your activities. The logs VPN keep on you might include your activity, IP addresses, connection/disconnection timestamps, devices used, as well as payment logs.

Any one of the above elements would give you a little less anonymity because your actual IP address can be linked to a particular log. Of course, even when the government has the log, it is still difficult to tie this to you unless they try hard enough.

In short, the fewer logs the VPN provider keeps on you, the better.

However, there is one more thing you need to keep in mind: Never trust the ads. While their sales material may say that your privacy is guaranteed, it is the privacy policy that counts in the court of law. So go through their privacy policy and see what data they keep on you.

Using VPN And TOR

While VPN and Tor are different, you can use both of them together to enhance your anonymity further online.

You are forgiven for assuming that Tor and VPN are the same things. However, they are not. You see, a VPN is a network of company-owned servers that protects your privacy through the encryption of your data packets and IP masking to prevent online monitoring. Here, your VPN provider has control over both the VPN client on your computer and the servers that you connect you. Therefore, it is crucial that you choose a VPN provider that you trust. On the other hand, Tor is a network of servers owned by anonymous volunteers across the globe. No one on the network is associated with each other in any way, shape, or form other than the fact that they are volunteers. No companies or organizations own both the Tor browser and the server in the Tor network, and you do not need to trust any particular individual to handle your data because the route your data goes through is chosen at random. Because of this fundamental difference, you can use VPN and Tor in conjunction to further enhance your security because your data would go through to a VPN server and appear at a location far from yours and go through three random nodes before arriving at its destination. The best part? Your data is encrypted several times throughout the entire process. So unless your attacker has some very serious firepower at their disposal, they can do very little to your data.

Of course, there are downsides to both VPN and Tor, and no one can say which one is better. Tor is good because it is completely free, although it tends to be slow, and compatibility is a major problem. VPN is faster, but is limited in protection potential, as previously highlighted. Using both of them would mean you would need to spend money, deal with the security weakness of your VPN, and deal with the compatibility and speed of your Tor browser. But at the end of the day, you are more protected than 90% of the world population.

But that is enough theory crafting. How do you use both Tor and VPN? Well, start by downloading the Tor browser from their website and install it if you have to. Then, launch your VPN client and choose an exit location somewhere outside your country. At this point, any connection from your computer will go through your VPN provider servers. From there, launch the Tor browser like you would with your ordinary Internet browser. Once open, click the connect button, and you are good to go.

At this point, your connection is secured by both Tor and VPN. Of course, you will need to deal with slow connection speed because of all the redirection needed to get your data across to its final destination. But hey, such sacrifices are necessary to protect our privacy.

IP Leaks And Kill Switches

Kill Switch

A kill switch does what it says on the tin. The moment your connection has been compromised and protection is no longer guaranteed in any way, shape, or form; the kill switch will literally kill your Internet connection and block all activities until a safe and secure connection has been reestablished.

A kill switch is an important feature to have in your VPN. It protects your data whenever it detects suspicious activities. If your VPN does not have a kill switch and when a connection problem arises, your computer may attempt to reconnect to the site using the standard, unprotected connection, so it exposes what you have been doing.

IP Leaks

IP leaks are a common vulnerability depending on people's setup when they surf the net. One cannot put the blame solely on the VPN for this problem. IP leaks occur when your VPN cannot hide your real IP address when you are surfing the web. For instance, suppose that you want to watch a YouTube video that is geo-restricted, meaning that it is unavailable to you in your country. Many people can bypass this by launching their VPN client, select a different exit location, and then go back to the video. It should then be available. However, if you do that and the content is still blocked, that means your IP address may have been leaked.

Many VPN service providers are aware of that, and they have been working hard to minimize this risk.

Again, it might not be your provider's fault that your IP has been leaked. In some cases, it is because of how you set up your computer or some applications in your device. In fact, even the Internet browser that you use, or its add-ons, can cause IP leaks.

When To Use A VPN

There are many reasons why you should consider using a virtual private network to protect your connection:

1. Your activity online is encrypted

2. Your online activity is hidden

3. Your location is hidden, which allows you to access geo-restricted contents on YouTube, Netflix, or other sites

4. Makes you more anonymous online

5. Keeps your connection secured when you use a public Wi-Fi

Of course, all VPN services are free. Some of them, such as TunnelBear, offer a free trial, but it is very limited. However, all providers offer good prices, amounting to little more than 5 bucks a month. That is hardly any more expensive than a few cups of coffee. So really, you hardly pay anything for better privacy protection.

When Not To Use A VPN

There are really no reasons why you should not use a VPN unless you cannot make ends meet if you have to pay for VPN services. Other than not downloading dodgy documents from dodgy sites, not sharing too much of yourself online, using a good antivirus program, browsing sites that have secure SSL protocols, and basically being cautious online are some ways you can protect yourself online. When you add VPN into the mix, your security is bolstered even more.

How To Set Up A VPN

Setting up a VPN is very simple. First, you need to find out which VPN provider is good for you. TunnelBear and ExpressVPN are known to be good VPN service providers. So go to their website, create an account and choose one of their pricing plans and make your purchase.

Then, download their VPN client and install it on your computer. Launch the client and log into it using your VPN account. While different VPN clients have different ways to establish a connection, it should be pretty straightforward once you launch the client. Some of them, such as TunnelBear's VPN client, give you instructions on how you can establish a secure connection with their servers when you first launch the client. All you need to do is to select an exit location, which is the location of the server you are connected to thinks you are connecting from. Just make sure to select a location outside your country and click connect. With that, you are all set up to browse the Internet, feeling a bit safer.

Tor Vs. VPN

If, for some reason, you do not wish to use both Tor and VPN, you may be wondering which one to use. Well, it depends on what you need.

As mentioned previously, a VPN ensures your anonymity by redirecting your data through the provider's server. There are 4 main benefits of using a VPN:

• Encryption: All of your messages and data are encrypted as they go through from your computer to the VPN server before arriving at the destination. That means your ISP cannot spy on you, gather your data, and sell it off. This is very important in a country with a lot of censoring or when you need to send sensitive data such as your banking information.

• Speed: While your Internet connection is slightly slower when your data has to pass through a VPN server, it is still much faster than what Tor could provide. In fact, the difference can be so minuscule that you may not even notice it.

• Ease of use: VPN applications are straightforward and user-friendly. Anyone with a computer can install and use it.

• Compatibility: Some of the best VPN providers out there have extended their services from computers all the way to mobile devices and home router.

However, there are downsides to VPN:

• Weak encryption: Depending on the VPN service provider, the encryption strength may not be as good as you may be led to believe. Never accept anything less than military-grade encryption.

• VPN software failures: The VPN software needs to be reliable because it is responsible for encrypting your data going out of your computer. If it crashes for some reason, your computer may switch to sending unencrypted, unprotected data. For this reason, many VPN providers install a kill switch that would cut off all connections from your computer when your VPN software fails.

• Different logging policies: This is something that we have previously covered. Basically, you need to understand how your provider logs your activities, so read the privacy policy carefully. The rule of thumb here is that the lesser information they keep on your activities, the better.

Tor, on the other hand, wraps your data in multiple layers of encryption, which are to be peeled off at each intermediary nodes before arriving at its destination. There are two reasons why Tor is better than VPN:

• Hard to shut down: Unlike a VPN that is run by a company, Tor is comprised of thousands of servers across the globe. Shutting down any one of the servers would do nothing, making Tor very difficult to shut down. It does not have a centralized structure like VPN, so there is no specific place the government can attack to shut Tor down for good. Because Tor servers are run by volunteers, you need to find each individual server and shut it down one by one. While you are doing that, you can only hope that more do not appear. So you see, it is impossible to shut Tor down.

• Near-complete anonymity: While Tor is not completely invulnerable, the people working on the Tor Project are constantly updating and making Tor generally harder to breach. There is no such thing as 100% anonymity in this day and age, but at least Tor can provide you 99% of it, which is better than even the best VPN.

However, Tor has some downsides, including:

• Slow connection speed: By default, your data is required to go through at least three nodes or more. That means a lot of redirecting, encryption, and decryption. As a result, expect to see very slow connection speed. Using it to watch videos or upload/download documents is not going to yield a very pleasant experience for you.

• Volunteers: Since the entirety of the Tor network is run by volunteers, there is no built-in way to provide financial support to maintain and upgrade the network. Certain servers are outdated and slow or have poor connections. Moreover, there is the possibility that some volunteers within the network are not trustworthy.

- Low compatibility: As of now, Tor is not available on iOS, which means that you cannot use it on your iPad or iPhone.

Tor And VPN – Which Should You Choose?

To help you decide, here is a quick list of features to help you decide before we go into the details:

	VPN	Tor
Connection speed	✔	✘
Compatibility with all devices	✔	✘
P2P File Sharing	✔	✘
Complete Anonymity	✘	✔
Protection of All Online Connections	✔	✘
Price	✔	✔
Easy to Set Up and Use	✔	✘

Access to Support Team	✔	✘

Consider Using VPN Over Tor When:

A VPN is a good privacy protection tool for casual users who just want to protect themselves when they browse the Internet. VPNs can protect their users' data, including backing information, shopping behavior, torrenting, accessing blocked contents, among others.

When you browse the Internet, your ISP and other third parties are collecting some form of data on you. An unprotected connection is an open invitation for an interception, which can reveal sensitive information that you happen to be sent at that moment, such as your login information. Therefore, you should use a VPN to protect yourself from such attacks.

A VPN is highly recommended if you use public Wi-Fi often because they are notoriously unprotected even though they are widely available. In fact, the equipment needed to hack into such services can be obtained very easily. If you often travel and to countries with a high level of censorship, then you can never go wrong with using a VPN.

Use Tor When:

You may have already guessed this, but not many people out there use Tor. Most people get enough protection from the VPN. So why should you use Tor? Tor is best when you just do not trust VPN to protect you. It does not guarantee complete anonymity, remember? So if you are an undercover journalist writing a report about the atrocity committed by your own government, then the stakes are high indeed.

In such cases, your life could be in danger. While some attackers may be able to get through a VPN protection, all you will ever lose is some of your private information. However, only a few organizations have enough resources even to attempt to track you down when you are using Tor, and when they do manage to track you down, your fate is in their hands. So you definitely want to have all the protection you can get.

Other than providing you with complete anonymity, Tor is also free, and easy to set up and use.

In short, VPNs are for casual use to keep you safe online. However, if you really need to go dark, then Tor is your best bet.

Chapter 5: Enhancing Your Security Using A VM

VM stands for Virtual Machine, which allows you to simulate a computer inside an application on your computer basically. Think of it like running a computer inside your computer. VM can simulate an operating system that is so lifelike that attackers tend to have a hard time telling if your machine is a real one or a virtual one. With VM, you can run software that is incompatible with your system, try out other operating systems, or run applications in a safe environment.

There are many powerful VM out there so anyone with a computer and an Internet connection can set up their own VM. You just need to download a VM app and go from there.

What Is A Virtual Machine?

Let us take a step back for a second. Before you start to use a VM, you need to know what it is and how it functions.

You see, a VM app simulates a virtual environment. Simply put, it creates a virtual machine that functions and behaves exactly like a computer. The VM app runs as a process in your operating system, and you can boot an OS into the VM, and it would think that it is being installed into an actual computer as mentioned previously, VM functions and behaves like a normal computer. That means it will run smoothly as any other PC would.

For the sake of disambiguation, we shall call your computer, which is running the VM "host" and any OS running inside the VM "guest(s)."

The best thing about VM is that you do not need to partition your own hard drive to get VM to work.

The VM creates its own virtual hard drive to store the guest OS. Again, the guest OS would be tricked into thinking that the virtual hard drive is real.

As you have already guessed, running a computer inside a computer does have its own downsides. For one, the virtual machine cannot run as fast as the host machine because the latter has to dedicate some resources to simulate a virtual computer. That means if you want to run some demanding games or other applications that are resource-hungry, don't expect to get some amazing performance out of it. That means you will not get a good performance out of your MacBook when you use it to run Windows PC games unless the games are old, or it is not as resource-hungry.

Another amazing thing about VM is that you can have one of them running on your PC at a time, so long as your PC has enough resources to run all the VMs. The most limiting factor is your hard drives because VM does require a huge chunk of it to store gigabytes of guest OS. If you run multiple VMs at the same time, expect to see some performance drop because each one of them requires some resources from your CPU, GPU, RAM, among others.

Advantages Of Using A VM

Other than to satisfy your tech geekiness, VMs have many useful applications.

For one, you can install and play around with other OS to get a feel for them without having to install it on your hardware. For instance, you can experiment with different Linux distributions and see which one is suitable for your needs. When you are done experimenting, you can just delete the VM. It is as simple as that.

You can also use it to run other software that is exclusive to certain operating systems. For instance, if you want to run Window-exclusive software on your Mac or Linux computer, you can just use a VM to run the software. If you use Windows 10 but wants to use applications that only work in Window XP, you can install Windows XP into a VM.

Another reason is for security purposes, which is why VM is mentioned in this book. You see, VMs are sandboxed from the rest of your system. That means all the applications installed in a VM can only interact within the VM, so they cannot do anything to your host OS. Should the application behave badly, you can just delete the VM, and the badly-behaving application will vanish completely. For this reason, VM is a perfect place to test apps or websites that you don't quite trust and see if they are the real deal.

This has been a bane to many tech support scammers out there. If you go to YouTube right now and write "Tech support scammer virtual machine," you can see what those people can do to your computer. But thanks to VM, they are powerless. The VM stops those people from accessing your sensitive information and documents.

Speaking of security, if you wish to run unprotected OSes in a controlled and safe environment, you can do that with VM. So when you need to run a Windows 95 application, you can just install that OS into your VM without the risk of compromising your entire system.

How To Set Up A VM

Before you can start to set up a Virtual Machine, you need first to choose a VM program. There are many out there, such as VirtualBox, VMware Player, VMware Fusion, and Parallels Desktop. However, it is recommended that beginners start with VirtualBox first to get a feel for VMs. VirtualBox is compatible with Windows, Linux, and Mac OS, but it is rather basic in what it has to offer. It is a good starting point because it is free and is an excellent tool when you want to use VM to protect your data. From using VirtualBox, you should be able to develop certain tastes and needs that you can use to identify what other VM programs you should use because they offer many more features compared to VirtualBox, albeit at a price.

For the sake of simplicity, let us start with a clean slate. That means making the assumption that you have no experience with VM at all but is tech-savvy enough to know your way around the computer. For this purpose, let's start setting up a VM using VirtualBox as, again, it is the best option for beginners.

Start by downloading and installing VirtualBox. After that is done, launch VirtualBox and click on "New" to create a new VM. A window should pop up asking you what OS you want to install. There should be a name box that lets you type the OS name, so go ahead and type it in. The installation wizard will attempt to guess which OS you wish to install, but if your selection doesn't come up, then click on the dropdown menu and manually select the OS you want. When that is done, click "Next."

You will then be taken to the next screen. Depending on the OS you wish to install, the installation wizard will automatically select the default settings for you. But you can always change the settings on the following screens. You have to decide how much memory you want to allocate to the VM. You can change the value as you like, but if you cannot decide now, don't worry. You can always come back and change the settings later.

The wizard should then create a virtual hard disk to support the guest OS in your new VM. Select the option to create a new virtual hard disk file, unless you already have an existing one that you want to use.

Your next decision is whether you want a dynamically allocated or fixed size disk. The former means that the maximum disk size is set, but the file in there will only reach that size as needed. If you choose a fixed size disk, then the file created will be just as big from its creation.

It is highly recommended that you go for fixed-size disks because of the increased performance even though the files will take up a little more space. Moreover, you know how much disk space you will use anyway and won't be caught by surprise when the files in the VM start growing.

Next, you will be asked to set the size of the virtual disk. You can choose the default value or change the size to what you need. Once done, click "Create" and the virtual hard disk will be created.

You will then be taken back to the VM main application window where you started. The only difference this time is there is now one more VM in the list. Before you start, make sure that the installation media you need to install the OS is available. This often means putting an ISO file or a disc and then go to the VM's setting.

Once all of that is done and dusted, you should be able to run your new VM now. Just select it and hit "Start."

Chapter 6: Freenet Specifics

What Is Freenet

Freenet is similar to Tor for the fact that it is created to address privacy concerns. Its creation can be traced back to Ian Clarke, who, with the help of other researchers, created a system to guarantee anonymity on the Internet in 1999. This feat is achieved by encrypting a user's data or content, chop it into countless snippets, and then distribute them across other users' computers. Therefore, in order to obtain your data, you need to connect through all the intermediary computers that pass on content requests.

Similar to Tor nodes, other users' computers cannot access your data because Freenet uses caching, powerful encryption, and decentralized structures. Ever since 1999, Freenet has been under continuous development.

Freenet functions as a P2P network that is self-organizing and utilizes unused disk space across countless computers in its network to store snippets of data, therefore forming a collaborative anonymity system.

Thanks to its decentralized structure, the Freenet network is robust and has no potential for single failure points.

However, it is worth pointing out that P2P environments are generally unreliable, and their users should not be trusted. That means that all users in the network are expected to fail without warning or that they are operating maliciously. In order to prevent failure or malicious activities, the Freenet anonymity tool employed various tactics to protect users' data.

Here, each user is assigned a node that they run. This node provides the network with some storage space. When another user wants to add a new file, they need to send an in-network inset message that contains the file. The message is then given a Globally Unique Identifier (GUID) that is dependent on the location. That means that the file is distributed across a set number of nodes.

The files uploaded do not just stay in one place, either. They may be replicated or relocated over time. This is where Freenet really shines because even the node containing the file snippet is offline, there are other nodes to extract the necessary data from. Another advantage that Freenet has is that no particular node is responsible for handing a huge amount of data, so even if a node becomes compromised, the attacker would gain little value.

If you want to download a file, you need to send a message with the GUID key. When the key reaches the nodes that have the files, the node will send the data back to you. Thanks to data encryption and request relaying, it is hard to determine who uploaded the content into the network and who downloaded the content.

How Is Freenet Different From Tor?

While Freenet and Tor provide anonymity, Freenet is an in-proxy network whereas Tor is an out-proxy network. That means you can use Tor to access the Internet and the dark web if you so wish, but you cannot use Freenet to browse the open Internet because the anonymity it guarantees is self-contained.

That means Freenet is its own Internet. It hosts its own websites, messaging, file sharing, and email platforms as well as other services.

Vulnerability

As of now, I do not recommend you use Freenet because law enforcement agencies have claimed that they have successfully infiltrated Freenet and managed to reveal the users' identities. However, no technical details have been given thus far. As far as we know, law enforcement agencies have a presence in the Freenet as well.

Chapter 7: The Invisible I2P

In this chapter, we will take a look at I2P. We will discuss what it is, its strengths and weaknesses, how it squares up with VPN and Tor, as well as how to set it up in a simple and easy to understand way.

What Is I2P?

First off, what exactly is I2P? It is the Invisible Internet Project (IIP or I2P) that is built using Java but on similar principles to Tor. It is a decentralized and anonymous network designed from the ground up, intended to be its own darknet.

Simply put, I2P is an Internet inside the Internet. When you are connected to I2P, you can perform online activities such as sending messages, browse websites, create blog posts, communicate with forum members, and more, anonymously. Of course, you can surf the larger Internet using I2P, but it is not really designed for the job, and you are better off using other application for that purpose

I2P is primarily used to share copyrighted material or data because it is very unsafe and illegal to do so on the open Internet. You can do that thanks to I2P anonymizing networks. It allows for torrenting through I2PSnack, which is a torrent client created specifically for I2P.

In fact, I2P torrenting is becoming more and more popular nowadays. Of course, that does not mean that I am condoning torrenting. The purpose of this chapter is to discuss its usage in the context of staying anonymous online.

Another client on I2P worth mentioning is I2P Bote, which is one of the two main messaging services on I2P. I2P Bote allows you to message other users anonymously through a secure network. That means you cannot send messages if you are connected through an unsecured network. Messages sent using Bote are automatically encrypted, making it one of the most secure communication solutions out there.

How To Use I2P

If you go to the I2P official website, you can tell immediately that their resources are for those who are very tech-savvy. Ordinary users may have a hard time understanding how to use it. Not to worry! Although it is impossible to explain things in simple terms, we can at least tell you how to set it up in this very brief guide.

So, if you prioritize security, then you need to use Linux distro, especially a security-oriented one like Tails or Liberté Linux. You should not use Windows or Mac OSX. However, if you really want to take it a step further, you can use Ipredia OS, which is a Linux distro OS based on I2P itself and all websites and services are only accessible if your connection goes through an I2P proxy tunnel.

How To Set Up I2P

First, go to the Java official website. Download and install Java. This is because I2P is built using Java programming language. Therefore, you need Java to run it. More often than not, your computer should come with Java already preinstalled. If not, then you just need to download the latest version and install it.

Next, go to the I2P official website, download and install I2P. When you launch I2P, you will see a console window. If you do not know how to proceed from there, you can copy and paste the log files from here, which will be needed for those who help you set it up.

You should also see a browser window open on the I2P Router Console page. It will let you know that you have connected successfully to the I2P network. If it doesn't show up immediately, don't worry. It can take a while before the I2P software starts to establish secure connections. After having established a secured connection, the Router Console will let you know that you are now fully connected.

I2P Browser

You need to configure your browser properly in order to browse websites on I2P. Again, you can find out how you can configure your browsers such as Firefox, Google Chrome, or even Internet Explorer so that you can use them for browsing I2P networks.

There should be a guide for every Internet browsing software. Because Internet Explorer is insecure and Chrome opens you up for surveillance from Google, consider using Firefox. Whatever browser you chose, the process should be similar.

First, go to Firefox. Click on Options, then Advanced tab. Go to Network Tab, then Connection Settings. Find the "Manual proxy configuration" box. Then enter these values:

HTTP Proxy: 127.0.0.1

Port: 4444

Consider adding 'localhost, 127.0.0.1 to the 'No Proxy for' box. Click on "OK" and go back out of the Settings. Your browser should be set up now.

If you use Firefox, consider using FoxyProxy, which is a Firefox extension that helps change proxy settings quickly should you use I2P frequently. The only downside is that you may experience connection problems.

Now you can start to connect to I2P websites, which are called websites. They have the .i2p suffix, unlike .com or .org or other suffixes on the surface web, or .onion from Tor websites. Don't know where to start? Consider navigating to the I2P Router Console window. You should be able to find some I2P links to help you familiarize yourself with the new Internet dimension.

VPN Vs. Tor Vs. I2P – What To Use

Now, the big question is which among the three is best to use? Why not all three of them? You would be most secured that way. But if you want to use only one of them, then it depends on what you want to do online.

VPN is fast and easy to use, perfect for general Internet browsing, and if you are not a tech geek. VPN provides enough privacy protection against most online attacks. At the very least, I recommend you use a VPN all the time.

Tor adds another layer of protection, and I highly recommend it if you absolutely have to browse the Internet anonymously. For instance, if you are a political dissident and want to contact a journalist to get the words out there, you can connect to Tor through a VPN.

I2P is a better option if you want to browse the Dark Web. While it is not as famous as Tor, it does its jobs well and offers better speed compared to Tor.

Chapter 8: Tails

What Are Tails?

The Amnesic Incognito Live System (TAILS) is a security-based Linux operating system that is designed to protect your privacy right out of the box. For one, it protects its users by routing all connections through Tor, and every non-anonymous connection is blocked by default. In order to use it, you need to boot it using a DVD or USB. Unless you configure it to leave footprints behind on your computer, it will leave no trace.

Tails are funded by the Tor Project to support its development. Tails are not for everyone because it is designed for people who come under aggressive and targeted surveillance. If you are not one of those people, then you may have no need for this operating system.

History

Tails were released in 2009 as the next iteration of the Incognito, which is a Gentoo-based Linux distribution. The Tor Project, the Debian Project, Mozilla, and the Freedom of the Press Foundation are known to be funding Tails. According to Barton Gellman, Luara Poitras, and Glenn Greenwald, they used Tails to communicate with Edward Snowden, who was an infamous National Security Agency (NSA) whistleblower.

Why Should You Use Tails?

Tails are one of those OS that is the easiest to set up because it comes with many security applications and software pre-installed. However, as mentioned previously, there is no need to go through all the trouble of downloading and installing another OS that is based on Tor unless you know that you are under active and targeted surveillance.

Chapter 9: How To Safely Enter The Dark Net

With all of that in mind, how do you get into the Dark Net safely? Thankfully, you do not need to be a tech geek to access this safe haven. It is a safe and simple process. In order to enter the dark web, we recommend that you follow what we call the "Super Onion" setup because it prevents other people from knowing who you are, then attack your computer, then steal your data.

Why Super Onion? Because it has several protection layers with the OS at the front, then your surfer account, then VPN, then Linux, then the Tor browser itself. Before you get into the think of it, it is worth pointing out that you need to be at least computer savvy. Still, even if you are not, you should be able to do just fine with our guide.

Another thing worth keeping in mind is that nothing is 100% safe. Even tech giants such as YouTube, Google, and Facebook get hacked. With enough resources and time, nothing is impossible to hack. However, with all of these layers of protection, you can at least deter most hackers out there. Other than that, the methods we show you here are not intended to help you escape law enforcement.

Finally, make sure you follow our instructions every step of the way. Do not skip or alter any steps. Otherwise, you risk making your system vulnerable.

Secure Your OS And Create A Surfer Account

First, make sure to update everything on your computer, including the operating system and the applications. From there, check to see if your firewalls are enabled.

Next, turn on full-disk encryption so that your data will not be leaked into the virtual machine that you will use shortly. Use strong passwords for all OS accounts, with symbols, uppercase, and lowercase, numbers, etc.

Disable auto-login. Then, create a non-administrative account on your computer. Call it whatever you like so long as you know that it is your surfer account. This account shall be used just for diving into the dark web. Whenever you are in this account, never visit your own websites or type out your name, or do anything that might reveal your identity. Be very careful with what you type when you are on this account.

Set Up A VPN

As mentioned earlier in the book, Virtual Private Network allow you to hide your IP and location in case an attacker manages to break through your defenses and gain control of your virtual machine.

Here, it is worth noting that setting up your VPN using public Wi-Fi is actually better for the protection of your privacy. You can skip steps 2 and 4 and sign up with your real email and credit card if you believe that the VPN is not going to get hacked or if you prefer convenience. However, I strongly urge you to follow these steps as you can never be too safe.

So, here is what you need to do:

1. Change to another account if you are currently on your surfer account.

2. Create an anonymous Gmail account such as "Anon007@gmail.com" Any other reputable and free email providers work as well if you do not want to use Gmail for some reasons. Make sure never to enter your real information when you sign up. If they ask for your phone number and you cannot get past this step, then you can choose one from [receive-sms-online.info/] or one in this site

[raymond.cc/blog/top-10-sites-receive-sms-online-without-phone/] to receive SMS verification online.

3. From there, select a reputable VPN. ExpressVPN or TunnelBear are good options. NordVPN got hacked in 2018 but only spoke up in 2019, so it is probably not a good choice. Sign up for the VPN services using your anonymous email address. You may need to make a purchase if you want to get the most out of these VPN providers, though.

4. You need to pay anonymously, so you can go to [privacy.com] and sign up with your anonymous email address. You can then generate a credit card number and use it with an arbitrary name and address as you proceed to the checkout. The only downside is that privacy.com still needs to use your bank account number, so there is a small vulnerability here.

5. With an account created and services bought, log off your current account and log back into your surfer account.

6. Download and install the VPN client. Before you connect to the VPN, make sure to select an exit location anywhere that is outside your current country. Halfway across the globe is usually a good idea.

Install Tor Browser On A VM

In comes the Tor Browser. For an added layer of protection, you need to run the browser in a virtual machine. So, do the following:

1. Log into your surfer account and connect to the VPN, making sure you chose an exit location outside your country.

2. Download and install VirtualBox.

3. Download and install Debian Linux as a virtual machine. You can find the instructions on this handy   site: [networkworld.com/article/2937148/linux/how-to-install-debian-linux-8-1-in-a-virtualbox-vm.html]

4. Make sure to use a very strong root password. Again, use numbers, symbols, uppercase, and lowercase characters.

5. From there, go to VirtualBox Menu, then Machine, then Settings. In the settings, disable hardware acceleration, serial ports, and shared folders. If they are already disabled, good! Keep them disabled. You might need to restart the virtual machine before the changes take effect, so do that just to be safe.

6. In order for the Tor browser to function properly, you need to match the VM time to the time of your exit location on your VPN. You can

change the time by simply clicking on time at the top of the screen.

7. Finally, select the onion icon at the top left corner of the screen, click on Security Settings, then set the security level to "High."

And that is pretty much it! You are set and ready to go explore the dark web! Well, not quite. There are a few more things to keep in mind to protect your own safety.

Dos And Don'ts For Your Safety

Do:

• Launch everything in this exact order: OS, Surfer account, VPN, VM, Linux, and then Tor browser. That means you must not launch VM before setting up your VPN. Otherwise, you risk compromising your own safety.

• When you are done browsing, close everything down in this exact order: Tor browser, Linux, VM, VPN, surfer account, then OS.

• Consider taping your webcam and sealing the headphone jack with tape or 3.5mm jack with its wire cut off.

Don't

• When you are on your surfer account, do not do anything else other than getting your VPN and VM set up. That means not surfing the surface web using Google Chrome. Also, do not enter any personal information or even type anything about you in your surfer account, especially in your virtual machine.

• Do not share files between the VM and the host system (OS). If you must, you can use a USB drive to share files, but you need to format the flash drive before and after transferring the file. Unless you know what you are doing, opening files you get from the dark web is never a good idea.

• Do not put the VM on pause or switch from your surfer account to other accounts. If you must turn everything off as described above before switching accounts.

Keep in mind that you are never 100% safe, but with all of these layers of protection, you should be able to deter 99.99% of attackers who want to steal your data. Unless you have something really good that's worth taking; no one is going to go through all that trouble of hacking you.

Chapter 10: Why Your Data Isn't Private, Even If You Don't Use Social Media

Some people have the impression that they are safe from spying eyes if they do not use social media. They are aware of their own privacy issues mainly because of numerous privacy breaches in the past. Based on this information, you would think that you are safe if you just don't use Facebook, Twitter, or other social media, right? Well, not really.

According to a study from the University of Vermont, coupled with numerous other studies in the past, there is more evidence than ever to support the argument that your privacy is no longer in your hands, even if you deleted your social media account.

To make matters worse, researchers from UVM's Department of Mathematics and Statistics published a report on Nature Human Behavior highlighting that users on social media reveal much of their behavioral data and that of others in their social circle.

You are forgiven for thinking that because you have never used Facebook or other social media platforms before, you are perfectly safe from online surveillance. Well, that is true if you have no friends or family. If you do and they use social media, then the chances are that social media companies know more about you than you think.

Researchers gathered over 30 million posts on twitter from 14,000 users online. To ensure accuracy, they excluded retweets and bots or other non-personal accounts. With over 30 million posts, they can populate their model and begin to study how much data they can extract from a person based on his or her tweets. They did not use keyword-tracking by using language modeling or just quantify information within a certain time frame. Instead, they use what is called information-theoretic tools, which combine structural and temporal approaches to allow for a clearer understanding of a user's online persona. Moreover, researchers looked at the user's most frequent Twitter contacts to see what other data they can extract from the user as well as to predict future tweets from the user. Through their studies, they managed to compile enough data about a person than what the researchers expected to get.

Further extrapolating the data from just 10 of the user's contacts, researchers managed to find out more about the original user himself. Researchers said that they could predict future tweets from the original user with about 65% accuracy. Even the data extracted from the user's contacts alone allowed researchers to predict future tweets from the original users with 60% accuracy. So really, even if you delete your account, your peers will continue to generate information about you and quite accurate as well.

What does this tell us? The study shows that information from just 10 people in your contact gives enough data about you that companies can predict your behavior in the near future. Of course, there is a limit to how much predictive information social media can have on you because there are certain things that you just will not say online. However, those would bother to profile you will know plenty of things about you. That includes companies who try to get you to buy their stuff to government agencies who want to study the population.

While these organizations or agencies cannot know everything about you, but they know enough to influence you and sway your attitudes. Things like political opinions or religious affiliations can be altered.

From this study alone, researchers discovered how vulnerable our privacy really is. You can be certain that someone out there has a folder containing all of your information, such as your likes, dislikes, political affiliation, and more. With this information, they can start to influence the way you think and talk.

If you think that no one has any data on you because you do not use social media, then think again. Your data can still be generated by those close to you. It takes a lot of resources to accurately predict someone's behavior, which has never been online before, but big companies such as Facebook or Twitter have enough resources to do just that. These companies can create a profile of you and can even use the data they have on you to track or even sell your data.

Data Access Methods

So how do they access your data and profile you so accurately? Well, there are many ways to do that. Take Flickr, for example. It is a social media platform that allows you to share geotagged photos. That means when you share a photo there, you also show your exact location at that moment. Using the photos alone, anyone can tell where you are visiting or staying. Geotagged photos make tracking your location or where you are heading easy for third party users. Phishing is common, both as a way to gather data and a problem in the workplace. Phishing reveals sensitive information through links or downloads through a simple click in the mail, messages, etc. Thanks to social media, hackers have more ways to get information.

Share It With Third Parties

Many social media platforms such as Facebook and applications such as Farmville actively collect their users' information and sell it to other companies. While Facebook's privacy policy explicitly says that they provide data that companies cannot trace back to the users themselves, Facebook violated this policy. So when you click on an ad on a page, Facebook will send a link to the advertiser who would lead them straight to your profile page. So it is very easy to identify who clicked on the ad. Facebook has faced scrutiny because Cambridge Analytica collected users' data without their permission. Users took a psychology questionnaire from Cambridge Analytica, but then it collected more data on the users themselves. They access the users' data and that of their friends. While the data collected may not be illegal, the data has been used to sway political opinions.

API

Application Programming Interface (API) allows all software to communicate with each other in your device. It is a set of protocols, routines, and tools to help software developers build an application. Through the use of query language, data sharing between applications and communities become straightforward. API accomplishes this by limiting external programs to have a certain set of features or permission. So APIs can define how a program interacts with everything else in the device.

Another use of API is data gathering. This is an enticing solution for researchers because it collects data anonymously, meaning that while personal data can be collected on a massive scale, none of the data collected can be linked to any specific individual.

However, thanks to the recent scandal of Facebook and Cambridge Analytics, API is now faced with scrutiny as well. You see, Facebook allowed third-party developers to create applications that are intended to gather data from their users. Though API, the developer managed to exploit a loophole and gather a lot of data from Facebook users without their knowledge.

Search Engines

We have been using search engines in our day-to-day life. Going through each and every website to find what we want is daunting, which is where search engines come in. All you need to do is type keywords into the search box, and the engine will find relevant sites for you. As long as you typed in the keywords correctly, then the results should be accurate. The only problem here is that some search engines keep track of users' data, and some may lead users to malicious sites that may steal the user's data.

Location Data

Another way users unknowingly share their personal information is through the use of location data. You see, many social media sites allow you to

115

share their geographical data through voluntary check-in apps such as that on Facebook. Other applications ask you to grant them access to your location, such as Google maps. So when you post something, as in sending data, you also attach with it your geographical location. In some cases, your device or application may send out other information such as OS language, device type, or timestamp. So that means whenever you post something, you share a lot of your information than you think.

Privacy Concerns

Nowadays, it is becoming clear that the right to privacy is one of the most fundamental human rights, especially in regards to freedom of speech.

Social Profiling

There is a law dated back to 1974 that prevents companies from disclosing your information without your consent unless the situation calls for it. To know more, you can go and read about the Privacy Act of 1974.

But basically, no entities (that means companies, organizations, or government agencies) are allowed to share your information with third parties unless you give them permission to do so. Unfortunately, under the principle of "presumption of innocence," it is up to you to prove that the entity had indeed disclosed your information. This is why all applications you have downloaded on your phone, as well as major social networking sites like Facebook, ask your permission before you can use any applications.

However, the Privacy Act still has exceptions. 12 of them, in fact, and they allow social media platforms such as Facebook to gather your information and then filter advertisements to certain demographics. Given the fact of how easy it is to give our more information about ourselves than we think, we need to take a long hard look at how social media sites such as Facebook or Twitter handle our data.

We already know that they store our private data, but what people may not know is that these companies also have access to the data as well. Those platforms are free, but you need money to host and grow it to this scale. Therefore, to make a profit, they provide personal information to advertisers. The data collected on Facebook, such as your likes, dislikes, or preferences, are very valuable to marketers. This allows marketers to personalize their advertisements to get better conversion rates.

Companies

Again on Facebook, there is only one way to ensure protection against apps that share your personal information. You can go to the privacy settings and turn off spam or otherwise unwanted apps.

Twitter goes through your phone contacts to allow you to find your friends on the platform. However, what they failed to communicate in the past was the fact that they also used it to learn more about you.

Instagram, after being bought by Facebook back in 2015, included a sneaky policy in their user agreement. Here, they gave themselves permission to use your own photos for ad purposes. You can find this policy in their user agreement, although it is very well hidden. You can opt-out, but you need to delete your account before a certain time. With this one policy, Instagram managed to fool a lot of people who had no idea what the company was doing. Thanks to this one clause, Instagram is free to disclose your personal information to third-party companies.

Institutions

Some institutions are becoming increasingly concerned about the lack of privacy for users using social networking sites. Those institutions include government agencies, schools, and libraries. Especially the libraries.

You see, there was a debate on whether libraries should allow their patrons to access social networking sites on the library's computers. The problem here is that libraries are committed to protecting their patron's personal information, and allowing the use of social networking sites that actively gather such information goes against their ethics.

Potential Dangers

Identity Theft

Because people tend to reveal so much about themselves online, it can be easy to fill in the gaps with what information you already have about a person. In fact, social security numbers can be inferred to facilitate identity theft. It has already been proven that you can guess, quite accurately, in fact, a person's social security number based on the data you extracted from their social networks and other online databases. Therefore, one of the ways to protect yourself here is not to share your social security number.

But identity theft is not just about stealing social security numbers. Just your pictures will do. Numerous cases have appeared in which users have their identity stolen because of their photos on social media.

Tragically, only a handful of people are actively protecting themselves against identity theft. In fact, it is very easy to acquire personal information from other people. You can get that on 1 million users for only $5. For this amount of money, you can get people's names, contact information, among other information.

Young People

Children and teenagers are the most susceptible online because they usually share more information than they need to online, which often leads to identity theft. While there are age restrictions mechanisms on various sites, their effectiveness is still debatable.

One of the main problems is peer pressure. Preteens and early teenagers are often pressured to reveal their personal information when they post something online. They often post quite a handful of content about their activities, thoughts, and opinions. They share such information not because they are expressive. In reality, they just do not want to feel left out or being judged by adults who are doing the same thing.

Moreover, teenagers feel the need to keep up to date with recent gossips, trends, news, etc. In their vain attempt, they open themselves up to cyberbullying and stalking. If it gets worse enough, they might just kill their opportunity at getting a job because they just cannot stop sharing private information.

This is a big problem because it is around this age when teenagers start to have relatively free access to the Internet, but they are the least educated on the problem of privacy.

Sexual Predators

Again, thanks to the increased rate of personal information being shared on social media, and the fact that it is very easy to create a fake identity, it becomes increasingly easy for sexual predators to operate online. While many large social networking sites are working hard toward combating this problem, how effective they have been is still debatable. There have been cases in the past in which children were kidnapped or even raped because they were lured out of the safety of their home and the watchful eyes of the parents and went to meet strangers they met online.

Stalking

It is now very easy to stalk someone online as well because social networks make it convenient to share your photos, contact information, interests, and location. This puts them at risk of being stalked online, and many users are not aware of this risk. There are numerous applications that allow you to do this with a few clicks. If you share your location frequently enough, someone out there can make a schedule of your daily activities. Who knows what danger you are exposed to when people know where you will be in the next hour?

Unintentional Fame

Sometimes when a user posts a funny joke, picture, or video, they become an Internet sensation. This can be a good thing if they go viral for the right reasons. If not, then this fame can actually ruin a person's life. It may jeopardize their privacy, chance of employment, relationship, reputation, etc. This is a clear violation of a person's right to pursue happiness. There have been plenty of cases in which unintentional fame has led the victims to take legal actions. A good example of unintentional fame is the use of memes. Take András Arató, also known as Hide the Pain Harold, for instance. What started as an agreement to become a model for some stock photos have led him to become a famous Internet figure. In reality, he never wanted to be famous this way, and he has considered legal action even though his ascension to fame has not negatively impacted his life. However, he decided to let it ride. It is good that his fame did not cause his life any harm. Imagine if it is the opposite. What would you do in such a circumstance?

Employment

As mentioned previously, unintentional fame can lead to unemployment. Sharing too much of your personal information is ill-advised if you want to have a good chance of getting a job. Back in 2008, CareerBuilder has conducted a study, and it shows that 20% of employers look up their potential employees' social media sites in order to screen them.

Most of the time, employers look for negative aspects or information about the candidates. For instance, information about alcohol or drug use, communication skills, the use of inappropriate photos, bad-mouthing other employees, or former employer, among other unprofessional behaviors. Only a small fraction of employers said that they chose employees based on their social networking profiles, and this is only possible because those employees displayed professionalism in their otherwise casual and personal profile.

While there have been laws and regulations to combat such discrimination, their effects have been minimal at best because any employer can craft an excuse and hire the next person. But the problem with privacy in employment isn't limited to recruitment.

Privacy issues are a major concern to those currently in employment. A quick search would reveal that there have been plenty of cases in which employees have been sacked because they posted comments on social networking sites that are considered to be damaging to the reputation of their company and their colleagues.

On the flip side, there is no law preventing employers from monitoring the activities of their employees. In fact, employers do not have to go through the trouble of monitoring their employees' activities online. There are monitoring services offered by third-party companies to monitor employees' online activities. An article posted by reading Write Web said that employers utilize such services to ensure that their employees do not disclose sensitive information to the public that may harm the company's reputation and put the entire business in jeopardy. But this is an invasive approach, and many civil liberties groups claim that just because employers could keep a watchful eye on their employees, 24/7 does not mean that they should.

Other than that, many companies out there employed certain monitoring mechanisms to ensure that their employees work continuously without stopping to browse websites during work hours.

Online Victimization

Victimization and other antagonizing acts are not that prevalent due to the direct legal and social consequences. However, social networks that are intended to facilitate communication among individuals over the Internet also open up new ways for certain malicious individuals to commit undesirable online social behaviors. This can negatively influence other people's online experience. Such online victimization can take the form of sexual advances and harassment, which are prevalent among teens and adults who are female.

Surveillance

In this day and age, many people are aware of how Facebook, Google, or other tech giants or social networking sites are collecting their data in one way or another. Everything you do online will be recorded and stored in a neat little folder containing every single information companies have on you. We tend to leave such cyber footprints behind that can speak volumes about us without realizing it. Thanks to all the data collected, it becomes easy to conduct social studies and achieve a better understanding of how we behave. While you may have less than 100 friends on Facebook, your audience is much larger than this because there are more than 100 people who can see your online activities. As mentioned previously, social networking sites collect every single bit of your information. Your activity will be logged even if you type "restaurants near me" on Facebook. One can even say that Facebook singlehandedly transformed the public into a behavioral experiment center because of all the data they manage to collect. To make matters worse, even if Facebook does not collect data that can be traced back to their users, one can infer the identity of a user based on a data set by cross-referencing other data set.

Law Enforcement Prowling The Networks

While the ongoing online gag about the FBI watching over every single individual on the Internet is getting old, they have a real presence on Facebook, Twitter, LinkedIn, or other major social networking sites.

A good example to showcase this is the arrest of Maxi Sopo. He was charged with bank fraud, but he escaped to Mexico and went into hiding. No one knows where he really was until he started posting on Facebook. To be fair, he was not blatantly taunting the US government because his account was private. The only problem was that his friends' accounts were not. Through the data collected by his friends on Facebook, he was eventually caught.

Since then, certain states and law enforcement agencies are starting to rely more and more on social media to help them conduct their investigation. Social media has become a valuable resource. While a subpoena is required in order for the agencies to collect private information, certain social networking sites such as Facebook allows officials access to their data if it helps with their investigation. Thanks to this, the police have been able to locate, track, and make arrests. Moreover, the use of data from social networking sites has been invaluable for law enforcement officials to conduct investigations and monitor gang activities.

In the United States, the Department of Homeland Security started using personal information from social networking sites to screen immigrants in the US. While this move from the DHS was announced, it was made rather quietly and faced little criticism, most of which from privacy advocates. However, little has been done to sway DHS on continuing using such data to screen immigrants. The government can use Social Media Monitoring Software (SMMS) to track your location as you chat with your friends online. It can create a database containing information relating to your relationships, networks, as well as associations. It can be used to monitor protests and identify the ringleader in political and social movements.

Mob Rule

Mob rule can be described as allowing the people on the Internet to decide the fate of a person. In a way, it can be online harassment on a large scale that is concentrated on a small number of individuals online. It is a situation in which control is within the hands of those outside the conventional or lawful realm. The term "Social Justice Warriors" or "Keyboard Warriors" are often associated with mass online harassment.

For instance, if a person were to make an inflammatory remark on a sensitive issue, they may face very brief jail time at best if they are even arrested for making such a statement in the first place. However, the real danger comes when the

133

Internet got involved, and the individual was put to trial by Twitter.

The individual could receive death threats and other harsh remarks from many people on the Internet, most of whom are strangers. In extreme cases, the person could be doxed, and their security is at risk. It could lead to unemployment and traumas. All of this could happen to a person, and everyone else that sent the mean comments to the victim would get off scot-free.

Location Updates

Many major social networking sites allow you to "sign-in" to a location, thus sharing with your friends where you are. It can be exciting to keep your friends updated on where you went on your holiday. In fact, you can look back at your old post, and you can recall the good times you had when you went to Thailand on holiday 5 years ago. However, you compromise your own privacy if you share your location online, as stated numerous times in this book.

Take Foursquare, for example. They created another framework that attempts to gather as much personal data from their users as possible. It is illustrated by the fact that while many users want as much control as they could on their location privacy settings, only a handful of them really checked, let alone understood, foursquare privacy settings. Therefore, think twice before you share your location online. At the very least, you should know how the website or social networking platform protects your location privacy.

Invasive Privacy Agreements

Another problem with social networking sites is its invasive privacy agreements. More often than not, they own all of the content you uploaded to the site. That means all your pictures, videos, and messages are collected and used even if you delete your account. Many private policy documentations often say that the website tracks their user's location and activities based on the device used to access the site. For instance, Facebook records its user's information such as their IP address, phone number, OS, or even their GPS location through the device the user used at the time.

It seems that private policy agreements are very long for a very good but malicious reason. No one would be bothered to read, let alone understand, the agreements. Fun fact, all the important bits are often at the end of the agreement because people tend not to look that far.

Reading A Privacy Statement In Terms And Conditions

It seems that many companies are doing their best to hide information pertaining to how they store and handle their users' data. At best, you can find their privacy policy on the landing page as a very small button. At worst? It's hidden somewhere deeper, and you have actually to go look for it.

To make matters worse, when there is an update in the services the company provides, you may get information about the introduction of new services or changes in existing ones. However, policy changes are often left unmentioned, and it is actually up to you, the user, who has to check the privacy policy often to see if there are any new changes.

Many social networking sites require their users to accept their Terms of Use policies, which often contain clauses about allowing the company to collect your personal data or share it with third-parties. Facebook, for one, is infamous for its active data collecting efforts. That is not surprising until you hear about the fact that they make it hard for you to deactivate your account, retaining your personal data even after you have deleted your account, as well as the fact that there have been numerous leaks of personal data with third parties.

Of course, no one wants to go through the trouble of reading terms of service and privacy policy. However, just like dieting people who read the nutritional facts, you need to go through with this if you want to protect your own privacy. So, what are some of the things to look for?

1. Ownership of data that you post

2. Data handling after the account associated with the data is deactivated

3. Notification of changes in the privacy policy

4. Location of the privacy policy that is effective

5. What happens to the profile page after deactivation

6. Reporting methods for breach of privacy

7. Duration of personal data stored

Of course, you need to gather as much information as possible by reading the entire thing. But no one has the time for that, so keep an eye out for the above when you scan through the documentation. The information pertaining to all 7 points should give you a good idea of how safe the social networking site is.

Key Points To Protect Privacy On Social Networking

Realize That There Are Always Threats

As mentioned in the previous chapter, it is impossible to protect your private data perfectly. There are those kinds of people who will stop at nothing to hack and steal your information. Keeping your privacy secure 24/7 is very difficult, if not impossible. What you can do here is minimize the risk of getting attacked by not partaking in risky online activities, downloading a legitimate antivirus and anti-spyware programs to protect your systems against the Internet.

Be Thorough All The Time

This is not that difficult, although many people tend to not bother with it. You just need to log out whenever you stop browsing a website. You can also make sure that your browser does not save your password. Not logging out leaves your accounts vulnerable to online attacks.

Other than that, keep your full name as well as the address to yourself. You risk putting yourself and those living with you in danger if their location is revealed.

Know The Sites

Make sure that you read the fine prints. Always. Many websites, such as Facebook and Instagram, encourage users to accept their terms and conditions that are best for the company, not the users.

You need to know what to do when the platform's security is compromised. We have covered how you can read the fine prints in the previous section already.

Other than that, make sure that the website itself is safe before you start sharing your information. You should not do it if you don't know who can have access to your information.

Moreover, make sure to familiarize yourself with the privacy protection of the website. You might need to take your time understanding how the site protects their users' privacy or how they use information collected from you if they do collect private data.

Protect Your Devices

That means encrypting your devices as well as your account. Use strong and complex passwords and change your password regularly (once a month should be good enough). When your devices get stolen, at least whoever took it cannot access sensitive information in there.

Another avenue of attack for hackers is to get you to download files and opening them to release viruses or malware and steal your information or install something that might compromise your device's security.

Be Careful About Taking Drastic Actions

There are certain actions that expose you to more risk of getting your personal data revealed. Be careful when you engage in the following actions:

• Adding a new friend

- Clicking on links

- Posting photos

Conclusion

In conclusion, the Dark Web may seem to be a thick forest populated by cutthroat bandits and criminals. However, upon closer inspection, it is a safe haven for everyone who wants to hide from spying eyes of the government, companies, or other malicious third-party who seek to manipulate and silence you.

In fact, the Dark Web is not only for political use. It has a place in legitimate business, as well. The Dark Web can be said to be the future of the Internet where everyone can speak their mind and find all the information they need without the fear of having their identity revealed.

The Dark Web offers the freedom that we all want. However, we should all keep in mind that anything can be used for an ulterior motive, and the Dark

Web is a prime example of that. However, anonymity itself is a blessing and a curse.

With it, anyone can speak their mind with impunity. This opens up the possibility of people harassing each other online without having to face the consequences. On the other hand, it allows sensitive information to be shared with those who need help, such as whistleblowers and undercover journalists. Government agents and innocent civilians alike are all concerned about their own privacy, so do terrorists. So, in short, it is everyone or no one at all.

However, experts on the matter are optimistic about the future development and growth of the Dark Web. If you are concerned about your privacy, then there is no better time to start protecting your own data than now. With all the information in this book, you should be well-equipped to start guarding your own privacy and enjoy a safer Internet.

If you enjoy reading this book and find that it has given value, please leave an honest review of this book on Amazon. We'd love to hear your thoughts on the matter.

Additional Resources

Chapter 1:

- https://www.thesslstore.com/blog/what-is-the-dark-web/
- https://en.wikipedia.org/wiki/Dark_web
- https://www.csoonline.com/article/3249765/what-is-the-dark-web-how-to-access-it-and-what-youll-find.html

Chapter 2:

- https://2019.www.torproject.org/about/overview.html.en
- https://trac.torproject.org/projects/tor/wiki/TorRelayGuide
- https://jordan-wright.com/blog/2015/05/09/how-tor-works-part-two-relays-vs-bridges/
- https://jordan-wright.com/blog/2015/05/14/how-tor-works-part-three-the-consensus/

Chapter 3:

- https://en.wikipedia.org/wiki/Onion_routing
- https://www.geeksforgeeks.org/onion-routing/
- https://blog.insiderattack.net/deep-dive-into-tor-the-onion-router-6de4c25beba7

Chapter 4:

- https://thebestvpn.com/what-is-vpn-beginners-guide/
- https://tech.co/vpn/are-vpns-safe
- https://us.norton.com/Internetsecurity-privacy-what-is-a-vpn.html

Chapter 5:

- https://www.howtogeek.com/196060/beginner-geek-how-to-create-and-use-virtual-machines/
- https://en.wikipedia.org/wiki/Virtual_machine

Chapter 6:

- https://www.darkweblist.com/2019/dark-web/freenet-another-secure-anonymity-browser/
- https://en.wikipedia.org/wiki/Freenet

Chapter 7:

- https://proprivacy.com/guides/i2p-guide

Chapter 8:

- https://en.wikipedia.org/wiki/Tails_(operating_system)

Chapter 9:

- https://medium.com/@deepwatch/how-to-enter-the-dark-web-safely-a-step-by-step-guide-819ba4e2cd6f
- https://www.comparitech.com/blog/vpn-privacy/how-to-access-the-deep-web-and-darknet/
- https://www.makeuseof.com/tag/how-to-access-the-dark-web/

Chapter 10:

- https://en.wikipedia.org/wiki/Privacy_concerns_with_social_networking_services
- https://www.forbes.com/sites/jessicabaron/2019/01/23/think-your-data-is-private-because-youre-not-on-social-media-think-again/
- https://www.purevpn.com/blog/what-is-Internet-privacy-scty/
- https://secureswissdata.com/Internet-privacy-issues/

Further Readings:

- DeepDotWeb: contains many useful resources such as news, tutorials, reports, forums, and more in the Dark Web.

- Tor Hidden Wiki and the Hidden Wiki: If you do not know where to start browsing the Dark Web, then you can start here as they serve as the unofficial directories for the Dark Web. Just be careful, though, because some of those links may be malicious or out-of-date.